SHEENAGH PUGH

Selected Poems

seren

Seren is the book imprint of
Poetry Wales Press Ltd
Nolton Street, Bridgend, Wales.
www.seren-books.com

© Sheenagh Pugh, 1990
    Reprinted 2000, 2004

ISBN 1-85411-029-2
A CIP record for this title is available from
the British Library.

The publisher works with the financial assistance of
the Welsh Books Council.

Printed in Palatino by CPD (Wales), Ebbw Vale.

Contents

New Poems

from Crowded by Shadows

from What a Place to Grow Flowers

from Earth Studies and Other Voyages

from Beware Falling Tortoises

Translations

NEW POEMS

M.S.A.

The news shows me more than I want to see.
I hold the *Guardian* between the screen
and my eyes; peer around at the Persian boy
coughing poison gas over his uniform.
I know with my eyes shut what he looks like:
dark smudged eyes, long lashes, skin
like ivory. That's how they look
in my memory, the ones who must be
sixteen years older now.

The camera slews round; shows women
shapeless in black cloth, and I go back
to the paper. One hidden face
is like another, and any one could be yours.

                She was twenty-three
                in Berlin: there was a busload
                down on a student trip
                from the north. (The Shah sent them
                West, to study science
                and be out of the way.)
                There were a dozen, all
                dark-haired, pale, willowy,
                but she was *die Perserin*,
                the only woman.

                She stood out anyway
                from the others; she laughed
                a lot. The boys didn't laugh;
                they were intense and pure
                and a little ludicrously
                serious, and very young.

Any of these young eager soldiers
tumbling like puppies towards death,
eyes shining, brain in neutral, could be them.

They're forty now, if they're alive,
but when that boy crouches miserably,
doglike, vomiting war, it's as if
none of them had grown a day older.

> That was a hot summer:
> we found a lake
> in the Zoo-park, and talked,
> while she held her long fingers
> in the water. They bowed down
> under the turquoises: blue
> roughcut masses; her dad
> traded in them, she said.
>
> She was going back
> to him, when she'd qualified
> as a textile chemist. The West
> was fine, free and easy; the boys'
> fiery purity passed her by,
> but he had a walled garden
> full of old roses, a house
> full of old books, and whenever
> she spoke of him, she smiled.

There are a kind of thieves that come by day
with dogmas, policies and manifestos
and steal your country when you aren't looking.

Before you know it, you've no pride
any more; immoralities are uttered
in your name; your consent inferred
to actions that disgust you. It's happened
to me, but at least I've a chance
to change things: I'm an exile only
in my heart.

Whenever I see fatherless,
landless people, living on sufferance
among strangers, lowering their eyes,
learning to adjust, their very language
drying to a trickle on the stones
of their throats, I hope you aren't there.

        The hotel room in Berlin
        faced east: the morning sun
        from Ulbricht's fortress fell
        on her dark fall of hair.
        It shone blue: gold glints
        of light like fish in the black
        water; she slept late
        of a morning.

        Talking half the night
        at breakneck speed,
        comparing options: Shah,
        Islam, Communism, like goods
        in a bazaar; spotting flaws
        in the fabric; rejecting
        the lot.... Asleep, she'd turn

                    her face a little in the light,
                    like a sun-worshipper.

I wish I could write your name,
but you might be safe
behind your father's wall, waiting
for better times, polishing the barrels
of your hidden mind, checking the cartridges
ready for action, like a good guerrilla,
and how could I send in the enemy?

The news shows me more than I want to see.
Whenever I watch some woman
behind a chador, scurrying for cover,
veiling her voice, I hope it isn't you.

                    Those boys...they believed
                    so much, it hurt. Their hate
                    kindled when they spoke of SAVAK,
                    the pliers, the shocks. It did sound
                    pretty bad, I said; she eyed
                    them from a distance: "Yes,
                    but they'd do it too."

                    There's a night club, called
                    the Cheetah; probably refers
                    to the price of beer. The Persian
                    boys drank coke, sickly-sweet,
                    innocent, just like them.
                    They looked askance at her
                    dancing: she laughed gently,
                    said things were changing.

                            14

They changed all right, I've seen them. I've read
about the squads of the pure-minded, keeping
the streets clean of unveiled women. I hear
they beat them on the soles of the feet.
Those boys were soft, frail; they'd surely flinch
from the sight of pain. Perhaps they close their eyes.

What happened in your country, when one
murdering old con-man replaced another?
How many girls hid their glinting hair,
their clear voices: how many sweet-faced boys
got a taste for torture? It's bad enough
he wastes their bodies in his wars:
firm flesh, straight bones, bright eyes, spilt
for a wizened bag of rheum. It's worse
that he made use of innocence; bought
ardour and hope at market in amounts
expedient to his needs. But the worst
would be if he insinuated craft
and hardness into their wide eyes,
made them like him.

Do not trust, above all men, Priam,
praising the seemliness of young men's
dead bodies; clinging to the altar
for his own life, when he ran out
of sons to send instead. He's cunning;
look how he conned Achilles, in all
his youth and grief, out of his revenge.
"Think of your old father", he wheezed,
"just my age, lonely for you".... Always

there are mooring-ropes: anchors drag
on the white lovely ship whose canvas
itches for the wind; who would sail so far.

> Her father behind his wall
> traded in blue stone:
> she lay under the wide sky
> melting in the sun.
>
> He traced leaf veins; touched
> flowers to his face:
> she analysed the fibres
> of silk, jute, glass.
>
> He stroked leather; fingered
> gold leaf on the page:
> she defended men's thoughts
> with soft-voiced outrage.
>
> He loosed the jesses; let
> his falcon fly,
> wherefore she returned to him
> most willingly.

The news shows me more than I want to see:
all over the world, young men blow off
young men's heads with guns people my age
have sold them. I'm not young any more:
it's the likes of me who counsel
compromise; who settle for less
than truth, because it isn't that simple,

who grow fat at the centre of a web
of coke pushers, or peddle nerve gas
to good customers and no questions asked.
I am the enemy now.

It was different after Berlin,
the free city. Back in the sticks
I checked my address book; climbed once
to the little flat in Bothfeld.
She was tousled, sleepy; it was only
ten a.m., but she let me in. I perched
on the warm bed, while she dressed
and looked embarrassed. Her body
troubled me less than this unease
of hers: for the first time
she seemed un-Western, distant.

And that was all, really. Not much,
except it was when I was young.
I can still see pictures, like snapshots,
not faded, but disconnected,
random: the blue light of turquoises
refracted in water; a face drinking sun;
the serious boys dancing together
to *El Condor Pasa*: I thought at first
it was backs-to-the-wall time,
till you explained they just liked moving
to the music, and they were too moral
to dance with women.
Now they perform together
on my screen the movements of combat,

as formal, but less graceful; it's hard
to keep the rhythm when you're dying.... But no,
of course, these aren't the same boys.
I was forgetting; we're all forty,
but I have no picture of you like that.
From all my shots you look out
undamaged, frank, bright-eyed, expectant,
laughing at the grave boys.

The Frozen Field

I saw a flat space
by a river: from the air
a jigsaw-piece. It is green
by times, and brown, and golden,
and white. When green, it gives food
to animals: when golden,
to men. Brown, it is ridged
and patterned, but when white,
a plane of evenness.

When frost touches it by night,
it turns silver: blue shadows
etch the hollows, grassblades glitter
in the grip of silence. It was
in such a place as this,
elsewhere, on the coldest night
of a cold winter, two boys
drove a car, with some difficulty,
over the frozen hummocks: parked
in the breathtaking chill, the stillness
that weighed each leaf down,
and shot each other.

It was a place I knew
years ago: I must have seen
the field, in summer maybe,
growing turnips, grazing cattle,
dotted with the white
of sheep, the blue and orange
of tents, and all the time
travelling toward one night
vast with misery; the sharp cracks,

one-two, like branches in frost,
that broke the silence.

Who knows what a field
has seen? Maldon sounds
of marsh birds, boats, the east wind.
The thin wail across the mudflats
is a heron or a gull, not Wulfmaer,
the boy who chose to die
with his king, never having guessed
how long dying could take.

And an oak lives
a long time, but a nail-hole
soon closes. Of all the oaks
at Clontarf, which is the one
where Ulf Hreda nailed one end
of a man's guts, and walked him
round and round the tree, unwinding
at every step?

The night the boys died,
their field was Maldon was Clontarf,
was Arbela, Sedgemoor, Solferino,
was every field where a moon
has risen on grass stiff
with blood, on silvered faces.
...Aughrim was so white,
they said, with young bones,
it would never need lime again:
better not to see
in the mind's eye Magenta,

that named a new dye.

It was as if the field
clenched all this in
on itself, hunched over
the pain of all young men
since time began; as if
every crop it ever bore
crowded in on it: barley, blood,
sheep, leisure, suicide,
sorrow, so much, its being
could not stay in bounds
but spilled out over space
and time, unwinding
meanings as it went.

They tangle around
the field's riddle now: *I saw a stage*
for pain, a suffering-space.
The fine mist of aloneness closed it
in the morning: at sunset
it was flooded with blood.

Thinking such things often,
we should see too much. I see
a picnic place, a playground.
My eyes half-open, I lean
against a tree; hear through the ground
children's feet chasing.
The sunlight shivers: *someone*
walked over my grave. I chew
on a stiff grassblade.

The haggard and the falconer

To make a hawk, he sits up and starves
with her; stays with her through the pangs,
the hooded blindness, the sleeplessness aching
in the bones: three days and nights. The effect,
oddly, is to bond them, as torturers
the world over could tell you. Afterwards
they're a team: she'll fly for him
and her own pleasure, wear his colours,
take food from his hand, save
her meat for him.

   There are some, though,
that will not, and until she flies,
he has no way of knowing. A haggard
is a hawk that takes no partner
and shares nothing. Her keen eyes watch
her own chance; the dizzy vertical stoop
from the air, that catches the throat,
is for her; the kill her profit
and her delight.

   So he sits,
light-headed, chilled with hunger,
watching her; awake wondering
what she is; whether he has her.
Some say a haggard is the fault
of the falconer; a want
of devotion; he mustn't fail her.
While she is making, he'll scarcely see
his wife: he went in briefly
two nights ago, before he started

the hawk. His wife, as usual,
lay unmoved, watching him
under her eyelids.

When he has gone, she gives
herself ecstasies, fetching, in the dark,
great raucous breaths, heart hammering,
bright-eyed, exhausted. She could show
him how, but she will not: her love life
needs no helpmate, and if you can fly,
why share it?

Inter City Lullaby

They're both what, nineteen? Their dark hair
flops: they've had a long day on the beer,
or the travel, sitting slumped in sleep,
each with his feet cradled in the other's lap.

Balulalow, beautiful tired boys,
and if I could, I would give you the choice
of where to spend your lives, and what to do:
you should not so be shuttled to and fro.

Newcastle United black and white
on their bags: they'll be in London tonight,
looking to find the streets paved with brass;
fairy tales are practical, nowadays.

Balow marras, balow canny lads,
and if I could, I would rebuild your trades
and let you play at home all seasons long
at doing what you liked, and being young.

Two stations back, they were talking about
the fair at Whitley Bay, while they ate
the food their mothers packed, just before
waving them off to look for their adventure.

Lullay innocents: lully, lully, lullay,
and if I could, I would make away
the witch: break spells, change the frog-prince's shape,
shut down the engine's noise to guard your sleep.

The Climate of the Country

Hereabouts, there seems something grudging,
austere, about spring. A young forsythia
unclenches a small handful of yellow,
bright and cold, against a white wall.

A robin sidles into the garden
after worms; my grateful cat flexes
winter-stiff skills; leaves only
skeletal elegance, memories of flight.

Only two job adverts today
in the post office. I just met the vet
at the butcher's yawning; he was up all night
saving some lamb, helping it make the weight.

Official briefing for ministers on the recent violence in the capital

As Ministers will be aware already,
the recent spring festival was marred
when a brief but violent incident occurred
in the church. The full facts are not easy
to establish, because accounts vary,

but it seems that on the day in question
certain persons with a licence to trade
on church premises, duly granted
by the civic authorities, were upon
their lawful business, when a young man

who had some objection to their presence
began vandalising their property,
(mainly currency and pigeons); eventually
driving them out with some violence,
(a whip was rumoured to be in evidence).

The man is a disaffected itinerant
whose motives are not entirely clear;
he is said to have called his victims either
'thieves', or, by another account,
'businessmen'. In either event,

for the Minister's interview our advice
is to focus on the clear contempt
for law and order; the arrogant attempt
to impose the whims of minorities
and the interference with private enterprise,

which might very likely have put
jobs at risk. A police investigation
should soon result in charges against the man,
who, though a minor youth cult, is not
in himself a serious threat, it is thought.

Uninhabited island

Those who go there now will find no men:
it's not a place for living any more,
just a stone expression, a landscape feature
in the sound; high and hilly, two miles by four.

There are two chapels and a burying ground
and ruins that were homes some years ago.
They built drystone walls, for want of lime,
and roofs of driftwood, since no trees would grow

under the galeforce winds. They grew barley
though, and fished, and kept sheep,
and there was a school, and men were born
and died here, their lives given shape

by these bounds; coloured by this climate.
It was hard, and they could not be less;
islanders are wreckers, and no doubt
their sleep was filled sometimes with the cries

of sailors, but that's all over now;
whoever sleeps here lies quiet enough,
and he who lands now from the sea's anger
will find no danger waiting, and no love.

The black ram

Last spring I saw where he had come
when I passed a field of white ewes,
twenty, perhaps, and every last one
had a black lamb. As patterns go,
it had class, the chess pieces
against the green.

What gentle contours this countryside
has: colours muted behind a glaze
of rain, like a tumble-polished stone's.
And somewhere in the pasture, hidden,
is he, the power-cell, alone now
with the vast pulse

of self that stamped his print so clear
on March, his landscape, the genetic
material of our map. The earth
should hum with him; his blackness
crackle; fizz along the unseen
live wires.

He'll feed alone; how could they let him
at the flock all year? He stores
his energy till two short days
of autumn light: then explodes
a blaze of black, recharges
the batteries of blackness

for another year. The quiet fields
contain him somewhere. When I think
of him, menace comes to mind.

This spring, flocks are not so white
as they used to look: patterns
are being altered.

Man getting hammered: between frames

Black hair soaked in sweat,
face flaming, he lights up
one after another: stares
with set eyes at the defeat
inside him. They call this pressure,
he calls it humiliation,
and it isn't over. He must go
out soon, and take some more of it:
smile when it's finished; tell
his tormentor how well he played.
And you could try saying
it's only a game, but he
wouldn't hear you for the hammering
in his head.

Exhibition

He's playing trick shots to entertain
the crowd, because the match finished early.
And why was that? He was comprehensively
hammered, that's why; he didn't win

a frame. Now it's all going well:
now it doesn't matter, he can knock
them in from anywhere. There's a wisecrack
from the audience; he looks a bit pale,

small wonder, but he's right in there
fighting back, turning the laugh, as if
no-one just hurt most of the life
out of him for some hours. He's a master

now, showing them how to do it,
the skills of which most of us just dream,
courage, class, humour. That's the game
in the end, and he's a player all right.

Filing the Queen of Scots

The Queen of Scots
lamented much, in her captivity,
her billiard table, impounded
during her travels.

Her impassioned request
through official channels
about the *table de billard*
must have paid off, at last,

because her dead body
was wrapped for burial
in the green cloth.

The Queen of Scots
was unusually tall
and slender: she must have had
a good reach.

Long-fingered hands; the best
for making a bridge.

The historian notes her taste
for risk, her misspent youth,
tut-tuts: files her tidily
under 'queens: bad'.

But every act of filing
is a choice, and sometimes, in truth,
a cock-up: she just belongs
under 'billiards players: early'.

The ballade of Sexy Rexy

When some old gardener gave a name
to a new rose, in former days,
he'd choose some beguiling theme
of far places or fair ladies,
some concord of comeliness
to please the mind in all respects: he
did not call it Daily Express,
Yorkshire Bank, or Sexy Rexy.

There's the Duchesse d'Angouleme,
Evangeline, the Prioress,
Ispahan, White Wings, Moonbeam,
Emily Gray, Irish Brightness:
sweet thoughts in a becoming dress,
nothing to club the ear or vex me
like Ma Perkins, Daily Express,
Yorkshire Bank, or Sexy Rexy.

Now money's the name of the game,
publicity's the new mistress,
and sponsors: names must please *them*,
and they don't want echoes of grace,
but what will be good for business.
That's why the catalogue directs me
to Allux, Sunblest, Daily Express,
Yorkshire Bank, and Sexy Rexy.

Send no more, Sirs, to this address:
their mere names give me apoplexy.
I can't find room for Daily Express,
Yorkshire Bank, or Sexy Rexy.

Hello

All winter, no weather kept him in:
he'd perch his thin frame, right-angled
with arthritis, on an old chair
out front, in the scrap of waste garden
he couldn't dig. Whoever passed his door
ran the gauntlet of "hello": not once,
but over and over, dogging them down the road,
as they quickened their pace; kept their distance.

However often the answer came,
it wouldn't be enough. It was as if
he were delaying the need to embark
on shipboard: as if the silent house behind him
were an ocean, and he standing in talk
on the quay, unwilling to leave behind
all the noise, the bustle, the harbour life,
and watch them slip out of sight and sound.

And now when the air has lost its bite,
and even in his garden, gold coins
of celandine gleam in the rank grass,
his door stays shut: has been shut
for days sliding into weeks. Unease
is starting to show now on the passers-by,
pausing, glancing at the drawn curtains.
If he is gone, nobody said goodbye.

Frankincense

The sweet gums live
in silver, locked away
in my vestry, till it comes time
to fill the aisles, the cold
high spaces with them. Even
their names went to my head:
resin and frankincense.

No-one slept. The gunfire
started before dawn. I went
to my church; prayed for the boys
from our village, and for the firing
not to come any closer.

About mid-morning,
the King's men nearly kicked
the door in. They had carts
piled high with wounded: all
our people that weren't dead,
and they just left them.

We laid them on pews,
their skull wounds soaking
into hassocks: all the bright colours
drowned in one. Their moans echoed
in song's space, and each day
the reek of festered flesh
crept higher, further.

They took them away
after a week. Women set
to scrubbing stone and wood,
while I burned all the incense
into sweet, dense smoke.

Now again the clean
empty, old-stone smell
fills the walls. At Epiphany,
when I tell my flock the coming
of the Magi, my guts clench
on one word, the stench of suffering.

Birmingham Navigation graffiti

By King's Norton is a long tunnel:
you take the barge in, looking back
at trees diminishing to a green pinpoint
of light. In the distance, another gleam
becomes a circle, a porthole, a tunnel-mouth,
and turns into Birmingham.

You see
towns' backsides from a canal. The tips,
the waste ground, warehouses, factory backs,
smoke-blackened walls, and all smothered
in fluorescent messages: *blacks out,*
Pakis out, shoot the Paddies, women
are all slags, gas the queers, fuck you.

Spray-paint spits in lurid colours,
jaundiced and gangrenous. One wall's bruised
an angry purple, one swallowed in flame.
Passing them takes forever: the canal
is silted with thick sludge, the discharge
of acid, scourings, waste.

                             Who is so busy
all these miles: whose bile spills so far?
Christ, can they all be at it: Irish
slagging off women, Rastas queer-bashing?
Towpath strollers start to seem a menace,
slouching, mean-eyed. You see them on bridges
and duck, in case. There's no safe mooring
this side of Wolverhampton, and all the way
the dark walls violent with magenta,

or sick with ochre. Steering through the scum,
like running in a nightmare, feet fixed,
toward the long flight of locks
out of the city.

                    Working through,
you don't pause for breath, till you edge out
at the last gate. It turns a corner
into open fields; there's a pub, people
chatting, walking dogs. The water's clear,
easy going: the wall slips by
with its chalky scribble of saxifrage.

Senesino/Farinelli

(London, 1734)

Calm down, Farinelli. It doesn't matter
that much. Come on now, hush.
That's it. What did you expect?
So his highness the Prince sits out front
and roars bravo, and comes backstage
to rave about your great voice?
And you turn up at his next party,
uninvited, and he shouts: "Get out, fellow,
none but gentlemen come here." Well he would,
wouldn't he? He only said you were a genius,
not that he'd let you over his doorstep.
It doesn't work like that. I should know,
I've sung here years, and my closest contact
with the aristocracy was the toe
of the Earl of Peterborough's boot.

Look at it their way. You and I
haven't so much as names. I'm just
the boy from Siena, no-one
in particular, while you borrowed the name
of the rich gent who had you castrated
as a kid, and gave you the lovely voice,
aren't you grateful? (Now *that* Farinelli,
they'd have let *him* in.) You can't talk
or dress like them...oh, you try,
and a right balls you make of it,
pardon the word. Now me, I don't bother.
Whatever I do, I'm still a street urchin
to them: well, that suits me. Urchins
can be as rude as they damn please,

(though it's wise to keep off the subject
of the Earl of Peterborough's mistress).

If it's any comfort, I don't think
it's much to do with what we haven't got,
—they don't treat the basses any different.
To them, any artist is less
than a man, and they're right in a way,
we're all stood here acting kings, heroes,
soldiers, never doing anything,
never truly being anyone.
They like to despise that, but also
they fancy it a bit, which annoys them
something rotten. Do you recall the time
we sang together, when you first came over?
We duetted first, then you took off
on your own, and I'm telling you,
you were magic. You rose cold and pure
above the music, above my jealousy,
above the worst troubles of each man
and woman out front. All their poxes,
their gambling debts, their adulteries,
their little meannesses, all washed away
on a great flood, and they couldn't hold it
back: they were crying, shaking, calling
your name.... Do you think they forgive you
next morning, when they come down from that,
when they're hung over, and not from drink,
trying to remember what sort of fool
they made of themselves: *Oh Christ, no,
I didn't kiss his hand?*

The least you can do
is not *turn up*, not then, in daylight,
looking so damned ordinary. They don't want
to see an over-dressed little man
with awkward hands and feet, and think: *he
did that to me; he forced my mind,
he made me feel, shout, cry*.... Be fair,
it's a bit much for a decent everyday man
getting raped by a eunuch. That's why
he had to screw your pride in return.
Don't give them the chance if you can help it;
don't enter their lives, just smile,
take the money and master them
every night from a safe distance.

Nothing happened here

Nothing happened here.
There was no demonstration: there were never
young people singing in this square,
and if there were,

they went home in good order, filing out
at the army's direction. Or if not,
then you could hardly wonder at what
you say they got,

though they didn't. Nobody died,
except soldiers in lightly defended
tanks, which were set upon, mob-handed,
by the misguided

counter-revolutionary anarchist
saboteurs (funded by the West
to ferment rebellion), who, as I stressed,
didn't exist.

Tree of pearls

Not hard like diamond: not even stone,
just the accreted irritant of an oyster,
a translucent accidental moon
with a strange pull for the lovers of power.
(It's the film queens, the brief mayflies,
who covet the rocks, the everlasting ice.)

But Ralegh at the top of the wheel
wore pearls in silver, the shifting moon's emblem,
and even he couldn't hold a candle
to a Cairo slave who went by the name
of Tree of Pearls, because the King her master
liked to hang the long ropes about her,

as if she were a white tree in bloom.
And at his death, not being in the mood
for a quiet safe life, she seized the kingdom.
Held it a while too: proved as good,
or bad, as all the rest: killed a fair few
of the innocent, and built a mosque or two.

But it couldn't last, and she waits now
in the citadel for the rebels to break in
and drag her out. She has something to do
before her bones are bruised blue and broken
by the wooden shoes of their slave-girls:
she lays out in circles all her pearls,

the worlds in which her light was reflected,
takes a mortar and powders each moon
to meteorites. *"Now it will be said*

no other woman ever put them on."
They hate to be outlived, the power-lovers...
"That will do: you may come in now, sirs."

The Chester Zoo marmot movement

He sits up, posing for Disney,
on his ample backside, and cleans
his fur. Seeing a cousin,
he squeaks delightedly and rushes
across for a kiss.

The little hills are laced
with their linked burrows. Faces
erupt each moment; high-speed visiting
breaks out again. At one end
of the enclosure their co-tenants,
the llamas, huddle apart,
frozen with distaste: Roman-nosed loners
trying to ignore the vulgar
camaraderie at their feet.

Fences make no odds
to the sociable sappers: they tunnelled
long ago to the next paddock
to perplex the bison. This year
an advance party is coming up
among the antelope: even
the tigers look uneasy.

There may yet be some hope
for things: I have a dream
that they dig right out into Chester,
Europe, the world, all undermined
with a network of kin, the neighbourhood
resistance, the underground movement
of love. I can see us standing

aside, wincing, telling ourselves
there's no such thing as society,
while the army of occupation
fraternises for dear life.

Reaches of light

The old man and his old dog stroll
stiffly, stopping to chat, often
resting. The last light of the sun
wells up: ribbons out like oil

in water. The vast sky is filling
from the west: a bright flood disperses
through winter grey; reflects in his eyes.
He is greeting someone and smiling,

passing on the light; his acts and speech
gentle, as ever. He strokes the dog's head
absently, like a lover. Gold and red
pale to pastels; rose, mauve, blue; reach

the far shores of greyness, as if there were
channels for colour, as if no edge of sky
could exclude it: a cosmic courtesy
to animate a face, or light a winter.

Sweet 18

You move before me with all the unknowing ease
of your age; your face clear of the awareness
that clouds mine. Your only scars: where you tried
to shave, before there was any need.
When you speak, shyness makes your words short,
and your hesitancy touches my heart.
It stands to reason I must want you to stay
like this: who could wish to make away
such innocence, such perfection?
Who has never wished to put a stone
through a great, clear, shining pane
of glass: who can see snow unbroken
and not long to crunch the chill of it
underfoot: to make their mark on white?
What is canvas for, but to take colour,
though the artist's thought is no sooner
fixed in paint, than it begins to fall
short of his hopes? You are a choice meal,
so perfectly set out on the plate,
that to disarrange one leaf, one floret,
would be to vandalise a gracious pattern,
but, for all that, I'd let my tongue learn
each taste and texture: the warm flesh juices
and the eyes' salt; the mind's crisp freshness:
I would leave nothing. I'd be ivy, resting
her lameness on the crutch of a young sapling,
using his life, sucking it out of him.
Think of me as old Mother Time,
your parasite, your predator: give her
a smile, glass of light, and stay clear.

Paradise for the children

This park's got everything. The flowered fan
around the pool is a landscaped garden
that shades into woods. Paths shoulder
through holly thickets to the high field
edged with trees, a green shallow bowl
with a dark rim, and from there you see all
across the terraced streets, over to Leckwith Hill.

It's a world enclosed, from tame to wild
in little: *paradise for the children*,
but it's parents who occupy the ring
of benches round the formal pool, gazing
at the bronze eternal boy in a glitter
of light, elusive in the leaping water,
his calm classical face teasing the spectator

with the hard make of youth, the unkind
perfection. The children seeking and finding
in the bushes hanker for their freedom:
given the choice, they'd leave mum at home,
but she compromises: sits out of their way
by the fountain, hearing them nearby,
glimpsing them through the gaps of light in the dark holly.

A bronze butterfly rests on the boy's wrist:
the frailest thing on earth, and the hardest.
She listens for their voices: too long
without them, she grows restive. They're younger
than they think: cocky, trusting.... That man
who was watching the ducks just now, alone,
where has he gone, and did he head in their direction?

Water splashing at the boy's feet,
he stands in a splintering of whiteness,
knee-deep in rainbows.... *They didn't listen*
when I told them stay together: where's that man?
The sound of falling water, the planted scheme
of colour, is meant to leave the mind calm.
How are you supposed not to worry about them?

The man strolls back, authority in his step,
admonishes someone...he's a park-keeper.
She laughs at her fears, feeling, for an instant,
paranoid and foolish.... But who says you can't
be an official, and a walking threat?
Teachers, priests, lawmakers have been that.
The naked boy poses on tiptoe, his bronze smile set

in mockery of Socrates and Plato
and all men whose wishes sink below
their words. *Did the sculptor's breath shake*
as he stroked your wax; indented your backbone
with his fingers? But you have been hardened
in the fire: no-one can put a wound
on you now, so unchallengeably young as you stand,

and will always stand, year after year,
while the beautiful children of men grow older
or get used and thrown away, like some
whose mothers dropped their guard for a moment...
...They wheel past, screaming like gulls: veer off
out of sight, shaking a paeony's ruff
into a brief red shower; echoing the water's laugh.

51

In memory of Annie Christina

Brave thief, bright-eyed
murderer, the birds
and mice will be wary
still, for fear of you.

Tumbler, comedian,
little vaudeville act,
without your wry face
laughter is less.

Sharp sight, sweet mover, why
was the blind machine
swifter, that took your life
and swept on, no wiser?

Quetzals only come once

The mother shakes the kaleidoscope,
holds it to the child's eye.
Swirls of blue deepen to purple
and black welling up. Silver flecks dart
through the shadows. She gives it a twist,
and a long path of light glitters
across it.

Ocean.

"Do another one".

She shakes again. Shafts of fire
filter through screens of brown,
red, orange.

Autumn.

"What else
can you do?"

She shakes again,
and detonates green. Patterns of jade,
lime, emerald, resolve
into a bird, a bright shiver
of greenness down its back,
its throat aflame.

Quetzal.

The child grabs: sends the pattern
splintering.

"Make the quetzal again!"

She shakes her head.

I can't:
quetzals only come once.

from CROWDED BY SHADOWS

Detour

(Gorsedd Gardens)

The shortest way here would be through the gardens,
just stretching now out of their crumpled sleep;
flowers on the bank and old men on the benches
tilting their faces to the pale March sun.

But he'll go round about, keeping the road,
for fear the sudden pigeons might fly up
in his face; for fear the old men's idle stares,
that miss no passer-by, should light on him.

Behind the low hedge he can see a sheet
of flame; cold daffodils, sweeping the ground.
A bird somewhere forces out its notes
as if they hurt; as if it were too small

to hold the music; but the man outside
will risk no pain, nor the eyes, nor the touch
of living things, nor come so close to light
that it might singe the edges of his sleep.

Guys

November light drains fast; the shadowed street
is littered with old men tacked clumsily
together from worn clothes. Most have been set
to beg for their child-masters standing by,
and plead from the obedient vacancy
of painted eyes. But sometimes, from some face,
real eyes stare out, seeing and ownerless,

begging on their own account. The children watch
resentfully these rivals canvassing
for pity, interlopers on their patch...
Apart from this, they are embarrassing;
tobacco, loneliness and spilled meths cling
about them. If they spared a thought for us,
they would expire somewhere more decorous.

But those that are of straw and sacking sewn
come to a merry death in sight of all.
Awkwardly perched, fun's focus, they take on
the shape of suffering; finally fall
among the ashes of the festival,
while children in a warlock circle turn
and clap their hands to see the old man burn.

John Howard

('John Howard' was the alias of Jesse James, shot in the back
while hanging a picture in his home.)

Your neighbours must have wondered what the town
was coming to; quiet, decent John gunned down
lending a hand about the house.... And when
they learned your name, what did they think, those men

with their safe futures? The name you put by
must have touched off many a fantasy
in armchairs where good folk yawned out their days
dreaming your dangers and your lawless ways.

But you lay under the vast stars and dreamed
of rooms, of fences, of being what you seemed
in your moments of escape; home-loving John,
as terrified of freedom as the next man.

'Industrial Landscape': L.S. Lowry, 1955

Where loneliness is, the sea is never far,
though here full of business; haphazard harbour
where shed and church and warehouse lie at anchor
and steam from factory funnels crowds the air

out on the distant sea-roads. People float
between the tall hulks; small craft, drifting litter,
a port's debris, and a mind's; the black matter
of melancholy, coughed hawking out.

Later he made real seas, empty of life,
not so much as a gull, and no longer
any people, as if his throat were grown harder
than to be fretted by the dust of grief.

The Partner

Out on stage, singing his song of love
to no-one in particular, his eyes
half closed, looking inward, he begins to move
in a grave dance whose slow intricacies

involve him wholly, and no other partner.
Circled in his arms, he acts out the caress
of the words; lets his hand wander on his shoulder,
under his shirt.... Step by step he betrays

all the trade secrets; makes the audience watch
the truth about all those who love in rhyme.
There never is a partner you can touch;
whoever writes the words, they are for him.

Inventory

(When Sir Walter Ralegh was committed to the Tower in 1618 an
inventory was taken of the contents of his pockets.)

Slowly he dredges up the glittering silt
from all those seas and years; a jacinth seal
of Neptune; sailor's luck, tied to a lump
of silver ore with a bit of frayed string,

another seal, with the old family arms,
a dead queen's diamond ring, a golden whistle,
a grinning god, an ounce of ambergris
and charts of journeys past; but the real chart

was this small heap of bright things, that might take
a boy's fancy, pleased with the new and strange,
or an old man's, careful of the keepsakes
time let him save out of its long wreck.

Delayed reactions

You saw this face for months; it never moved
you then; you never held it in your eyes.
One day you must have seen it otherwise,
because it had become the thing you loved,

and now no line, no look, but is uncommon,
chosen, apart. So quietly it grew
behind your eyes and entered into you:
to love it now seems only to be human.

So quietly works the sun on stone's hard face,
which first resists, but slowly drinks its fill
of warmth; turns golden, till it seems to spill
beyond its edges, blurring into space.

Odin

1. He hangs from the World Tree for nine days and nights to learn hidden wisdom.

MORNING

Soft red sun riding
pale waves; morning has come.
Light laps at my edges.

Earth's branches bear my bones.
I gave myself to myself
to learn what I was.

Frost stings the grass; a spear
probes me, sharp as the cold.
The pain searches me out.

Morning hardens the shadows
I have been in the dark,
where I was afraid to go.

My bones stiffer than branches,
I have tried death, and felt
the night inside me.

Morning shape, cloud-wolf
creeps toward me; I met him
in the dark spaces.

Morning shapes, clear-cut,
I have seen them otherwise;
I know where I have been.

Sun on the wood; warmth eases
into my bones; morning has come
nine times, and now the tenth.

4. He kills in battle those he has most favoured.

THE GUIDE

Yes, king, you have long had his love
secret and warm inside you when you drove
into battle, your face bright with a certainty
each man could light a candle of courage by.

He has filled your life and legend with his favour.
Do not think things will be the same for ever,
and when one day, turning to your charioteer,
you know suddenly who is really there

in the brief moment before he throws you down,
or see the old man, wolf-grey, coming on
through blood and metal to shatter the good sword
he gave you, do not begin to doubt his word,

or think you were lured here. It was the place
you would have come to anyway; he was
the guide who showed you the best way to go.
Now you are home, he has no more to do.

Spring '72

Now open flowers on the shirts of boys;
now mica glistens, asphalt's morning dew,
from pavements up. Now all the girls look pregnant,
and small red sports cars blossom on the streets.

Now all birds are not sparrows; now all women
unwrap their shapes from winter. Now the man
who thought it might be fun to walk to work
finds all sight aches, all touch troubles his blood.

Now all the state of opening, upspring, bud's
soft burst, a green grenade, scrapes at his grief;
now all the many dead dress him in black
for what they had and what he cannot keep.

Shoni Onions

He comes with autumn, when the leaves flake
from the rusty branches. His old bicycle
itself's a twisted tree, its creaking black
hung heavy with the long strings ripened full.
He is at the end of things; a sure sign,
the sad smile wrinkled in his golden skin.

There used once to be more of him, they spoke
a tongue that was the one half of a code
between old neighbours, a key to fit the lock
of cousins' speech, distanced but understood.
He sells in English now; his customer
or he mislaid the other words somewhere.

The boats that took our coal to Brittany
once brought him back; surely they don't still run?
Only old custom's sake now brings him by,
each year the same, a little older grown,
a taste sharp as nostalgia on his wares
startling the tongue; stinging the eyes to tears.

from WHAT A PLACE TO GROW FLOWERS

Grand larceny

For the two old men I saw
by St David's hospital
arm in arm; one blind, both shaky,
leaning on each other.

Do you know the story
of the king's fine fruit-tree?
Golden apples it grew; His Highness,
naturally enough, is scared stiff

of burglars, so he hires guards.
Ah, but who'll guard the guards?
He's thought of that too; one blind
can't see the fruit; one lame
can't climb for it.

You'll recall it didn't all go
quite to plan, because those lads
weren't daft, and soon worked out
that if the keen-eyed cripple stood
on the blind man's strong shoulders...

All honour to the wise thieves
who lend each other, in their weakness,
what they can, and manage to scrump
a few apples, a little happiness.

Coming into their own

I like to think of a day for all those
who have been unloved in legend; the crooked man
who married Morfudd, the mocked Menelaus,
Conchubhar, Mark of Cornwall, all whose pain

has been a good joke since the troubadours.
Always in the way, the comic hindrance
to the real hero; butts of tolerance.
Tristan had his day; it will come yours.

Stand up, sad, jealous, commonplace,
and make a flag out of the loneliness
you were supposed to suffer out of sight.
Embarrass us; make us admit to it.

Men growing flowers: Hveragerdi

(Hveragerdi; powered by natural hot-springs; major industry, fruit and
flower growing)

What a place to grow flowers;
a few houses clustered just under
a sullen, low-lying mist, sulphur springs
hissing from the ground, the shadow
of a mountain, strictly non-scenic.

And what growers of flowers;
these men, their faces ribbed
like the volcanic rock, the hard grasp
of their hands numbed of feeling.
It is these hands

that foster in the glass houses
the fragile ferns; these fish-eyes
that watch the colours spill
out of the calyx, the delicate shape
unfold itself,

and why, after all, should not
men in the bleak terrain
that makes their life, nurture
some bright thing; what a place
to grow flowers.

Ingthor the chanter

He is not like the other folk-singers,
the young ones with guitars and harmonies.
All he has is his raw, truthful voice.
He looks beyond the audience, his eyes

full only of the song, making the tune
in his head; nothing fancy, the words must enter
our hearts, and the notes must carry them there,
not interrupt them. Ingthor the chanter

has no art but the sureness of himself
and his country's old forms; easy in her rhyme
he moves without doubt or pretence. His luck
that he has her, and hers, that she has him.

The flute-playing at Skalholt

As the lady played the flute,
the notes scattered like water
from blessing hands;
as the lady played the flute,
the farmers came
in ones and twos, as if the sound
drew them from all about.

So quietly they came in
you hardly knew,
but look round, and they lined
the walls, hard-faced, hard-handed,
all in knee-breeches
and long red socks, and all
leaning back, lips parted, eyes
hungry for the music.

Einar, Gunnar, I wish you knew
your brothers Gwyn and Gareth,
who dress otherwise, but get by
much as you do, and on whom
may be seen the same light
of tenderness, when someone scatters
music over their lives.

The black beach

(Skogarstrand, South Iceland)

Nobody told us it was going to be black.
Day at the beach, see the puffins, fine,
and there it was,
   black.
   Not streaked with coal,
nor shaly, nor polluted; just pure ash

as fine as sand, running through our hands
and leaving no mark where we looked to see
a sooty smudge; uncanny, like a man
without footprints. The sea creamed in,

bone-white, startling; edging with lace
the black velvet. You could have sat down,
but no one did; no-one picnicked or made
sand-pies of the stuff. It was beautiful,

really beautiful, that stretch of darkness,
but people trod it as if they were walking
over their graves. A seal's shining head
surfaced close; seemed to look; then sheered off.

Going back to Hlidarendi

(Gunnar Hamundarson is leaving Iceland under threat of death, he
looks back at his farm, Hlidarendi, and decides to stay)

Did you think about it much,
farmer; no, you'd feel it
like a wave, wind sweeping the slopes
of wheat into a pattern
of light and dark, making
sense in your mind.

But you were right, no logic
could have led you better. What then
would going away gain you — your life?
Hardly, for death would come
to whatever place, and always
at an inconvenient hour.

You might as well await him
where your life is; in the place
that is to your liking.
A year elsewhere means so little
to you, with Hlidarendi
in your mind.

It is enough for you,
that wave; all the sea
you need; all your adventure.
There is a Hlidarendi
to most minds; on a map
sometimes, more often not; a way
to be.

Love

Bjarni drives the bus through fields of black
volcanic lava crusted with new moss
for visiting Americans who see
his country through the newest Leica lens.

Bjarni's eyes are never on the road;
at every moment they are wandering
to distant ice and skeins of falling water
and hills enamelled with small quiet flowers.

The land he shows the tourists every day
does not go stale for him; it hurts him more
all the time; its intimacy, its lovely
uncommonness. Bjarni tells his busload

about Gunnar, who to save his life
would not leave the slopes where his wheat grew,
the ones we are now passing on the right.
His voice shakes; he knows how Gunnar felt.

Eirik the Red

My son brought him. He was in a ship that struck,
and Leif picked up the passengers. I say
he landed us mixed luck; a good crew
of seamen and a mountebank priest
with a cringing whisper and butterfly hands.
This man talks to my wife, who followed me
from Norway when I had to leave in a hurry
because a few men got killed, and then again
when I had the same bad luck in Iceland.
And now she lives here at the top of the world
in this quiet white place, and no hardship
ever turned her from me — this man, I say,
tells her it is good to follow no-one
but the new Christ, and she listens to him,
and asks me, will I do the like. I say: No,
I will not say my father was a fool
and his gods nothing but empty wind.
She says then, she will not come in bed
with me any more, for her soul's sake.
Damn that priest for my cold nights
and my words unanswered in the dark
and the stranger who bakes my bread.
She's had a little church built, over the hill,
so that I can't see it from the window
or tell when she has gone there, but I know.

Swords

(National Museum, Reykjavik)

Swords don't keep well. The hilts are there,
and a scrap of blade, black and crumbling,
and a shape cut in cardboard, to show
what the rest was like.

In the next case are combs, coins, buttons,
all the trivial gear of a man's life; utterly
fascinating,

and still whole, with the marks of his use
and his love. But through the thing
that made his pride, I may not know him;

what made him a hero was less durable
than what made him a man.

King Sigurd and King Eystein

(From an incident in Heimskringla Saga: Snorri Sturlusson)

'When I went to fight in Saracen country,
seven times I had the victory,
and where were you, kinsman Eystein, then?'

Northwards in Vaage, building the fishermen
smoke-houses; they have work all seasons now.

'In Apulia I did not see you
on my crusade; where were you at that time?'

Setting up inns on the road out of Trondheim
where night frosts used to freeze the traveller.

'I saw Christ's tomb; I did not see you there.'

At Agdaness the ship-grave, I had made
a harbour, to save men's lives when I am dead,
and but for my life, it would be worse for them.

'What were you doing, brother, when I swam
the Jordan river, or when I tied a knot
by the bank, and promised my kinsman should come out
on that holy journey and untie it again?'

I was bringing under our rule the Jemte men,
not with war, but with good words. And a man unties
the knot he finds, kinsman, where he is.

Owl's night thoughts

(Edward Lear, talking to himself)

I like the night better than the day,
you meet fewer people. Even you, Pussy,
I'd rather think about you than be with you.
After all a poet, even a comic one
can make things differently to please himself;
iron out the abrupt answers, the casual hurt
you do to love as if it didn't matter.
Cats have claws, Pussy, and I haven't,
I am Athene's solemn, dull old owl,
trying to look wise and feeling slightly pompous
and very frightened of your glittering eyes.
Not that I want safety. I would rather
feel as I do, than not, and I will honour
beauty, although it burns me.... But you might try
not to make it worse than it already is.
Isn't it enough that we can never be
together; that I can never take your hands
and dance, or sing foolish old words to you
when your beauty catches me suddenly?
It isn't in the natural scheme of things
for owl and pussy-cat to fall in love.
They are too different; we...too alike:
there seem to be many ways to the same grief.
This world won't do, Pussy, we'll have to sail
to one where no-one has been busy yet
with laws like whom we shall and shall not love,
or putting guilt where happiness should be.
That's what makes us hurt each other; shame
and uncertainty, and blaming each other

for what we both want.... But in a place
where you could wear my promise openly...
I know, I know, it hasn't been invented,
but I'm a poet, Pussy, don't forget.

King Billy on the walls

I can remember looking up at him
on many a Belfast wall; King Billy, bright
in his chalk colours, riding a white horse,
larger than life, twice as victorious.

If I saw him again, perhaps I'd see
the sick, frail Dutchman with the tired eyes
who looked down on the drums, the exuberance,
the orange sashes, with an embarrassed air,

wondering when he became so popular.
And now he looks on fear and scattered flesh
and brutal faces, thinking of the years he lost
fighting the French, the Irish, his wife's father...

He was a gentle man, and all his life
a soldier, and now, trapped in the crude chalk
both friends and enemies use to picture him,
his eyes can still rest nowhere but on pain.

from EARTH STUDIES AND OTHER VOYAGES

EARTH STUDIES

Geography 1

We will look today at the island of Surtsey,
preserved for posterity on my colour slides.
Surtsey: off southern Iceland; thrown from the sea
in nineteen-seventy something or another
as result of volcanic activity.

Now here you see the terrific spray, the water
heaved aside as the rock was thrown up.
(Sea-water, that was; a shock of cold
when it struck you.) But the rock was still hot
with angry energy; it wanted to shout,

and here's where it told the world, erupting
that flood of colours, all triumph — look at the purple —
and gold warm and living as the sun.
(Look up the sun, someone, for next week.)

In this one the colours are cooling, which is why
the man can stand cautiously on the edge,
surveying the prospects. Surtsey was important,
because it was like watching the world begin,

as you can see here. The cooled rock, so black
after those colours, hardly bare any time
before the moss inched over. Even birds
nested in a few years. The man here
is a warden, guarding his little world

from any interference, letting it grow
as it was meant to. And there's a funny thing,
that men so carefully kept this corner
swept and dusted, while the rest of the house....

I saw it , you know. Surtsey. I saw it
one day in passing, it was a few years old,
just an offshore island, a stony outline
softened with lichen. Someone said
that's Surtsey, and I said: fancy that,
but I hadn't time to look properly.

The craft I left in was called Esau

The craft I left in was called Esau,
at least that name was scratched on the smooth door
I went in by. Someone said the engineers
gave them all names, I don't know. The stars
outside were what I noticed first; they looked
so incogruously normal. People joked
nervously; just like a plane flight.
They found seats, wondered if bags would fit,
gestured at the stars and told each other:
'Be seeing those in close-up soon'. No bother,
no big deal. I can't recall feeling sad,
not then. I think I was too interested
in the achievement, the technicalities.
And when we took off, there were the night skies
ahead; still, so still, a new ocean.
It seemed natural to look for an horizon,
as a captain would look where he was bound,
not back to port. Then the ship turned,
just slightly, and there was our long bright wake
already closing, and we looked back
along it to where you could still trace
charted coastlines on the bluish mass,
quite small really; uncanny with distance,
our late guesthouse; our inheritance.

Biology 1

The shapes of life were many; the double helix
never tired of inventing pretty patterns,
and even its earliest Meccano efforts
in sponge and coral were intricate beyond
fancy; a skeletal architecture
of lime and silica hulling the cell of life.

Then it all went mad; what else can you call
the kind of lavishness that provided
seven hundred thousand named insect species?
Why stop at one sort of opossum;
let's have seventy-six. Enough was never
as good as a feast, my most generous masters.

It will happen again, I suppose. The few plants
we brought; the white mice, will have the impulse
that explodes into difference. But it's like
a kaleidoscope; the patterns you shook out,
each with its singleness of line and light,
you will not make again, nor any man.

Biology 2

Where is Leviathan the humpbacked singer,
who stove the boats in his massive innocence?
Where are the eels who travelled to Sargasso
each year; such a long way to die?
Where the fine isinglass, the streaming bodies
apt to the seas' movement; where are the seas?

What is become of the dark bats flaking
like ash off the evening; what of the drifts
of butterflies? And the brittle-boned lords
of lift, calling, wheeling, balancing,
who had the freedom of the empty country.
Where are the sky's tenants; where is the sky?

Whose eyes now will see foxfur glitter
like quartz; who will hold the frail bodies
of moles? The garden is going back,
lovely even in ruin, but the stewards
are gone who knew what it once was
and whose memories were its only glass.

I think someone might write an elegy

I think someone might write an elegy
for the dead words: the shapely words
that have no shape to fit round now,
whose ladies have stepped out of them,
as it were, and left them in a huddle,
the words we don't have things for. I think
someone might write an elegy for words
like timothy, cocksfoot, feverfew,
fennel and saffron, ginger and galingale.
For mowdewart and marmot; for furze-pig
and parmaceti; for Lawrence the tod.
For cirrus, nimbus and stratocumulus.
For Persepolis, Hamadan, Shushan,
for Tolleshunt d'Arcy and Cirencester;
for Elizabeth Sarah Davidson,
which once seemed to me the fairest words
that anyone laid tongue to.
For the words that mean nothing now
and whose loveliness, made as it was
by what they meant, has left them; the husks
of dragonflies, drying out.... Things that are dead
we keep with words, but when the words die
themselves; oh then they're dead, and dead indeed.

Religion 1

A man and woman use
the freedom of a garden; a green bowl
filling with light; all stone, colour and cool,
perpetual surprise.
Their eyes can never rest, but on some thing
well-shaped; uncommon; fashioned to their liking.

They cannot leave alone;
though all is well, their hands still itch to do.
The leaf is not so seemly on the bough,
but they will have it down;
strip the bright branch to mend the nakedness
of their fair bodies; ever making good less.

At last the manor's lord
comes by and says: 'These gardeners will mar
what I most loved and trusted to their care',
(and that's a double word,
for nothing seemed to him so brave and bright
as they, when he dismissed them from his sight).

Of course it could not be.
It was a pretty tale; even believers
agreed they were a myth, the gardeners.
We should learn history,
which tells the truth, and makes old errors plain,
and helps us to avoid the like again.

History 1

In the beginning, they must have had ado
to know themselves different from the trees
or rocks; like infants becoming conscious
that toes and fingers are a part of them,
grasping the notion of a body: this is
the piece of earth that moves when I think.

Then other bodies: a forest of bodies
linked by tendrils of blood, need, liking.
Me, but not me. You, him. Them and us.
Mine.... It gets so tangled, after a while,
they make words, paths hacked out
through a thicket of possibilities.

It is long now since they saw themselves
naked; since they put the trees
at a distance. They drew a great difference
about themselves, until the paths they made
would no longer have taken them back home,
even if they had wanted to go.

History 2

So you have these hunter-gatherers,
as they were called, taking what they need,
what comes handy, and one day someone
discovers that you can depend on seed

coming up at a certain time and place
if you plant it; if you think ahead.
And for the beasts, they can be fenced in,
to be always there when meat is wanted.

A great step: men no longer have to follow
their food; bodies and minds are freed
to range or rest on their own chosen pasture.
For the first time since the earth was made,

it is for them; it serves their purposes.
Things can be ordered as convenient;
tomorrow mapped out, not left to happen.
In the background, a mountain smokes gently.

'Are you saying people got above themselves, sir?'

No, boy, nothing is as easy
as that. If a man comes across
something new in himself, you can hardly
tell him to put it back and mind his business.

Something made him think, puzzle, wonder;
whatever it was, he was stuck with it,
and it had its good side. How could you regret
that he had time to dispute some point of grammar

between hoeing turnips? What was in him
was what he had to be. It was a shame,
though, that the place where he ran out of room
to be himself happened still to be his home.

Geography 2

The land wrote itself before any
came to chart it: continents broke
and reassembled; two masses crashed
and threw a mountain range, a border
waiting for customs posts; glaciers cut
narrow valleys, close and separate,
each shuttered cautiously from its neighbour.
A coast curved itself into a haven
for shipping; a hill kept watch
on the landscape till the fort was built.
A river spread rich gentle living
over these fields; elsewhere, the want
of water made the contours stand out
like starved bones.

   And when it was all ready
they came, at last, to be masters
of it all; to take up the lives
mapped out for them.

History 3

I face him: I don't like him.
I hit him, he hits me.
We go on till one calls 'stop'.

I find a stick and make
myself stronger, but so does he.
Think of something else.

I sharpen the stick; shoot it
from a bow; he lies still.
I don't think I meant that to happen.

Now I fire lead; it makes
a mess and hurts, but I don't have
to see his face; too far off.

I drop death from the air.
I can't see him, but I know
he's somewhere hereabouts.

I sit at my desk and think of him.
I don't recollect now why we quarrelled,
but if he's calling 'stop', I can't hear.

Geography was peculiarly taught

Geography was peculiarly taught,
when I think back. I recall one year
at my school, we did the Masai tribe
of Africa: a people popular

with examiners, because they fit nicely
into half a term and aren't complicated.
I should say 'weren't', of course, but no matter.
Anyway, I remember how they mated,

dressed, hunted, built, but if you asked me
what weather, what contours shaped them;
what the land was like on which they happened,
I wouldn't know. And yet the lesson's name

was earth-writing. You would have thought the place
were a painted backdrop; the player's the thing.
If you want to learn, listen to the dialogue;
you don't look to the scenery for the meaning.

Religion 2

The first men thought of a mother: a vast lap
of green, bringing forth fruit, cattle, children,
sending out each to spend a day in the sun,
calling them back home when dark came down.

She would even make a king at seed-time
and reap him with the harvest; dig him
into the ground to be the new grain.
And he went willingly, so they say,

having loved her through all the seasons
of herself; having seen the winter light
and the opening; having done it all once,
feeling that next year could be no better.

Then came the Sky Father's people,
who saw more in a man than could be suited
by life, death, nothing; it seemed to them
beyond belief that they should cease to be.

So they rode out, par aventure, seeking
their fortune, wanting to know why
they were made, looking upwards, turning
to wave to their mother at the door.

'What do you think about heaven then, sir?'

I hardly ever do think about it:
if I need an excuse for sitting down
and resigning, there's always cowardice
or drink, which between them formed the best part
of my luggage. Nor could I, even canned out
of my mind, so cheapen the place I loved
as to think it a waiting-room. I was
amused, sometimes, to read all those poems
about the vale of miseries, and how much
the man longed to leave it. I always wondered
how those gents died; in a pleasant glow
of anticipation, maybe, or clinging
to the doorpost, pleading for another moment.
That's how I'd planned to go. I wrote my own
small poetic tribute to heaven, once,
for someone's child that was born dead;
it had been done before, of course,
but no matter. If you really want to know
what I think about heaven, the truth is
I think I lived there.

What Christie wrote when the child died

It is customary to write
that, having once opened your eyes
on our world, you reckoned it
a poor exchange for heavenly bliss
and transferred to the eternal side.
Thus may glib grief be pacified.

('It's for ourselves we grieve, not him,
for we are losers; he is none.')
But I say that you missed the time
of your life; your occupation;
the memories light owed your eyes,
which now are filled with emptiness.

Your hands were shaped to cup the fruit
that curved to them; your tongue was tuned
to taste the sour, the salt, the sweet;
your ears were shells where seas could sound.
For all adventure you were made;
to be anything, except dead.

Literature

You can find all the World's Great Works
in the central cassette library,
they brought the lot. Only the minor voices
were left to take their chance with the likes of me

in the hand luggage. I like minor voices,
semi-precious stones: I always preferred
moonstones to diamonds, and The Moonstone
to War and Peace. Which is why I cared

to bring the old horse Lyarde, and clerk Jankin
who sang the Kyrie to Alisoun;
the scholar who stayed to milk the ducks,
and dark Mary watching the sun go down.

All the unnamed voices, vibrant
with pleasure, fear, observation, hurt.
'Wher beth they, bifore us weren?'...
'More joy than there be stiches in my shirt'...

Only remember how accidental
is their presence; how many were the men
as pained, as joyful, who went down in silence
and will never be heard from again.

Biology 3

There was this term: natural resource,
which meant whatever might be put to use,
as: sheep, forests, phosphates, the ocean.
Parliament-men who wished to be in fashion
spoke of conserving, and avoiding waste
(translation: let's not use things up so fast).

It was assumed, you see, that things were there
to be used. Of course, conflicts could occur.
Say seals take fish: fish are food for men,
so kill seals. But we aren't philstine;
seals have fur and big eyes and therefore count
as a resource: the aesthetic argument.

It was seldom supposed, at least
by those who mattered, that something might exist
for none but its own purposes,
that one might be meant to say please,
as it were, before committing such a crime
as could not be mended: the theft of time.

After I came back from Iceland

After I came back from Iceland,
I couldn't stop talking. It was the light,
you see, the light and the air. I tried to put it
into poems, even, but you couldn't write

the waterfall on White River, blinding
and glacial, nor the clean toy town
with the resplendent harbour for its glass.
You couldn't write how the black lava shone,

nor how the outlines of the bright red roofs
cut the sky sharp as a knife; how breathing
was like drinking cold water. When I got back
to Heathrow, and walked out into Reading,

I damn near choked on this warm gritty stuff
I called air; also on the conjecture
that we'd all settle for second best
once we'd forgotten there was something more.

'Do you think we'll ever get to see earth, sir?'

I hear they're hoping to run trips
one day, for the young and fit, of course.
I don't see much use in it myself;
there'll be any number of places
you can't land, because they're still toxic,
and even in the relatively safe bits
you won't see what it was; what it could be.
I can't fancy a tour through the ruins
of my home with a party of twenty-five
and a guide to tell me what to see.
But if you should see some beautiful thing,
some leaf, say, damascened with frost,
some iridescence on a pigeon's neck,
some stone, some curve, some clear water;
look at it as if you were made of eyes,
as if you were nothing but an eye, lidless
and tender, to be probed and scorched
by extreme light. Look at it with your skin,
with the small hairs on the back of your neck.
If it is well-shaped, look at it with your hands;
if it has fragrance, breathe it into yourself;
if it tastes sweet, put your tongue to it.
Look at it as a happening, a moment;
let nothing of it go unrecorded,
map it as if it were already passing.
Look at it with the inside of your head,
look at it for later, look at it for ever,
and look at it once for me.

*

Harbours

There is the one you started out from,
and the one you were bound for, once,
but in between, there are so many,
mariner, that you stand a fine chance

of ending where you never had in mind.
You put in for repairs at some small port,
and the days go so gently, and the wind always
in the wrong quarter to make a fresh start.

Or there's a woman, or even a good inn,
something, anyway, that makes it seem
no great matter to get where you were going
when this will do as well.... All the same,

they stare out sometimes, your seaman's eyes,
over the glittering road you should have gone
to your true harbour. You shrug your shoulders
and settle for the less, like any man.

Sailors

Those of us who will never be sailors
catch sometimes, crossing a car park,
a breath of sea and openness;
for those of us who will never be sailors,
the market turns sometimes
to a milling harbour.

Those of us who were never sailors
recall Macao, Valletta, Port Mahon;
a name can bring us the sibilants
of strange speech, the scent of women.

Those of us who chose not to be sailors
go voyaging out, more often
than any sailor can, and our seas
are heavy with the death of friends
we never had; troubled with treasure
islands for which we lost
the map.
    In the old harbour
our sleep rusts quietly.

Old widowers

You can tell them, the old widowers,
chatting outside the supermarket,
then drifting apart as if they had
somewhere to go, but you know
they don't; they have all day,
the old widowers.

Their jackets don't quite sit straight;
their ties are the wrong colours.
No one inspects them now
of a morning; they're their own men.
They've slipped their moorings;

outward bound under no orders,
troubled only with freedom,
they hug the coast;
hesitate; stare far out
where the light flings down
its gauntlet of distance.

Lost on voyage

Bay of Portugal: boy seaman lost overboard
from the *Christopher*. Port St. Julian:
Robert Winterhey and Dutch Oliver,
the gunner, killed by giants. Here also
Master Thomas Doughty, gentleman,
and he was that all right, beheaded
for treason, and wasn't that a laugh,
only don't tell the General I said so.
South of Magellan Strait: the *Marigold*
lost with all hands in the great tempest,
twenty-eight men and Ned Bright, captain
and false witness; God wakes up sometimes.
Then in the islands, the pinnace
lost sight of in foul weather: aboard
Richard Burnish, Richard Joyner, Arthur
the trumpeter, William Pitcher, Paschie Gidie
and two men that served Mr Hawkins.
At Mocha: black Diego and Big Neil
the Dane, of Indian arrows; poor Tom Flood
and Tom Brewer, taken and eaten
alive in all our sight. La Herradura:
here we lost Richard Minivy, who faced
sixty Spaniards with his sword; more fool him,
but they needn't have cut his body up.
In the fight at Lima harbour, some man
called Thomas, shot from the *San Cristobal*.
Last, off the Cape of Good Hope,
one man, unnamed; we were getting a bit lax
with the log by then.

Other than that,
we're all fine; the ship's ballasted
with silver; we've all done more in three years
than most lifetimes hold. A fair voyage
with small loss, and he always paid our wage.

McGonagall's crucifixion

Then said Pilate unto Jesus: Why speakest thou not unto me?
Knowest thou not I have power to crucify thee?
But Jesus answered and said: Thou hast no power at all over me,
Except from above it were given to thee.

Oh...they didn't laugh. Kind of them.
In fact, I don't call to mind that anyone
ever laughed at that one. I must have got it right,
the Lord knows how: His be the credit.

I spoke of the famine in Hunan
to the sound of unseemly guffaws.
I urged pity for the drunkard's child
and the pub dissolved in merriment,
and when I described how those poor bodies
plunged off the railway bridge, all for the want
of buttresses, people nearly died laughing.

It was not the tragedy, you understand,
they were not so cruel; it was only
that I had not the gift to put it rightly.
You would not think a small matter of words
could unmake pity, would you?

My words trudged earnestly about their business
tripping each other up, stumbling
at every stone; my words could not dance,
could not move gravely to some measure.
They meant well; they meant mercy
and fellow-feeling, but it was not heard
for the sound of falling lead.

I really didn't so much mind
the throwing things: I could always dodge,
but it was like being a dumb man
all those years, to say and say
and never reach the ear; to have pity
shouting inside my head.

Oh...there was that once, of course,
that a measure of grace was granted
my words, by the Lord's good will.

The capon clerk

(or: complaint of a troubadour's lady)

A poet of love's a capon clerk:
remember as you read, sir,
and do not learn from him who crows
of what he never did, sir.

He is a man whose pride it is
to make excuse to suffer;
a man who hotly pleads for grace
and cools upon the offer.

He starves desire to feed his song;
he will be distant ever;
yet calls me cruel and murderous,
ungenerous of my favour.

The liar, he would not enter in
if I sent an invitation.
He'd rather sit outside the gate
and praise his hopeless passion.

He loves to paint his face with pain
and pose his shabby figure
where men may toss him sympathy,
like halfpence to a beggar.

He scribbles verse to my address,
to make my name remembered,
wherin his sorrows are rehearsed
and all his virtues numbered.

He loves his art; he loves his style,
his fame that will not die, sir;
he loves the scansion of my name,
but sure he loves not me, sir.

St Cuthbert and the women

He built them a chapel at the far end
of the island; they should not come in his church,
or near himself. And people said: a pity
the holy man should hate the women so,

and he watched them move,
far off, in their brave colours, bright
as illumined manuscript initials.
They sway from the waist like so many
flowers: if you go close,
there would be the same faint scent.
The stony island is watered
with their laughter, their chat about
some small happiness.

                    The sun sends
a shiver of warmth through him; voices flute
across; he wishes he were deafer,
his sight less keen, and that it were true
about the holy man.

from BEWARE·FALLING TORTOISES

The railway modeller

He's spent all week creating the best part
of a village; sculpting the paper strata
of its hills, painting them green, growing
small metal trees with a teased-out fluff
of foliage. Then he built half-timbered
card houses, secured them where they belonged
and stood back to be sure it was right.

Now he must add the people: so minute,
they take more work than anything. He uses
a make-up brush tapered to a hair
for touching their white plastic into life
with flesh-tones, bright splashes, uniform
blue and grey.... It takes hours to make
an individual, if it's done with love,

but he doesn't mind the time spent
in his shed, a sufficient universe,
and nothing brings a branch line alive
like people. Working down on the track,
picks raised, or waiting on a paper bench
for a train they can't board, they turn
the scene to a frozen photograph.

It's a shame he can't, with all his love,
move the frame on.... The background radio
intrudes news headlines into his thought:
today in Parliament the talking fellows
were voting on whether to punish men
with death. His brush carefully strokes in
blond hair; perfects another passenger.

In Memory 1: In Morriston Crematorium

In Morriston crematorium
he was burned with due decorum,

and he was scarcely thirty.
He left a wife, as they say,

and children too young to be grieved
or remember he ever lived.

He was not of decorous habits;
he should be out with his mates;

or maybe at a party,
anywhere but so tidy,

the quiet leavings of a man
stranded in Morriston.

In Memory 2: A Matter of Scale

He left no grief on Aldebaran;
Cygnus Alpha didn't know the difference
and the long lights of the Milky Way
never paled an instant for him.

Even on his own planet
the most people did not know him;
in his own country, his own town,
his loss was a small matter.

Only in a few lives
is a void left, wider
than a town could fill, or a planet,
or the great sun Aldebaran.

In Memory 3: Reallocation

No, I don't think they'll give us
a replacement. You know the boss;
if he can get three jobs done
for the price of two... Things'll go on
quite a while with you and me sharing
whatever work won't wait; leaving
the rest on that desk. About the end
of the month, we start complaining; he'll find
someone downstairs to do the audit,
the PAs get more letters to write,
and that's Ian sorted. In a week
or so, they'll amend the office phonebook
and send a notice round; you wait
till you see his name with 'delete'
against it; that's when you know
he's really gone. It's like an echo,
I always think: someone's been amended,
ended.

In Memory 4: Closing up

Things close up at different speeds: the space
you smash through the water with a stone

scarcely defines its edges before it's gone,
poured into; smoothed over featureless.

Or take out a rock-plant in summer
and watch the others ease into its room,
breathing out; making themselves at home,
till you could never put it back there,

because 'there' 's gone. And then a bike
skids, and a man is taken out,
and the edges of the long jagged cut
in people's lives feel so raw; look

so far apart, you'd think he would be missing
for ever, but they make new habits,
rearrange their world in a way that fits
one person fewer. That's the saddest thing,

when you can't see any more in your mind's eye
what used to go where the space used to be.

Magnolia

That time when trees, in particular,
are what they can be; bloom held close
still in a clenched fist of promise,
teasing you to guess at shape and colour,
nothing gives so little away in spring
as this tree, its wrought-iron ribs lifting

into an empty cup, curved space
where a tree will happen. Perhaps memory
and foreknowledge colour it for me,
invest it with quiet desperate grace,
or maybe it just is like that.
The others come discreetly; don't wait

for almond to flower, you'll be there all week,
but take your eye off this, and tomorrow
it's covered in wax candles with a glow
of warmth inside the whiteness, the like
of a young girl's skin, or an eggshell
full of some bird's life ready to spill.

And the first wind that blows, the first shower
slaps them loose; brings all that brightness down.
If the sun shines, a few days sees them gone;
even girls and birds have more staying power
than they do. The tree, iron again,
locks in its secret beauty, each year's pain.

Eva and the roofers

Eva in the back garden; a ton weight
of heat two inches above her,
palpable all around in the air,
her body on the grass blinding white
in all that sun and stillness. A whistle
shrills along some thread, invisible

in the light, some spider's filament,
and touches her. She looks idly back
up the sound's thin glittering track
to a roof opposite, and the glint
in the roofer's eye. He nudges his mate
and they call something, she can't hear what,

but the general idea's obvious
and she smiles to herself, satisfied
with the sun and the tribute. She puts aside
her book; shifts accidentally on purpose
to face a little more in their direction,
loosens a strap and starts stroking lotion

into her shoulder. All three play the game
as gravely as the steps of a gavotte.
('I look to be on offer, but I'm not'.
'We've no intentions, but a man can dream'.)
The garden, the fenced territory,
protects them all, wards off reality,

for while this one barrier's in place
they can let the sun melt every other.

Sex, class, reserve, duty, danger,
all *perhaps*, all blurred at the edges,
the way even people are when light
invades them so; arrows in, to commit

with so little respect, so gently,
an undressing of shape.... They work on at
their lives, while their minds float out
on an ocean of possibility.
They're singing; their skins drink sun; glow
from inside; they'll all burn tomorrow.

147

It's the magic number: seven more
than black despair, and that last black
has to be the hardest. He poises
his cue, and we all feel sick

with certainty: he won't make it.
That black is every job interview
we failed; every final step
we tripped on. It's every no

we heard when we needed to hear yes,
and it's going to happen again,
it's bound to.... There's the contact: too late now,
it's paused on the lip; we all breathe in,

and it's down, and everyone's going mad,
because destiny's taken a day off
and we've won. His laughter radiates
out at the audience; they mirror love

back to him, and everyone wants
to hold him, touch him, touch the luck,
in case it's catching. He did it
for all of us; he put down the black.

A short history of cocaine abuse

The soft snow that ate your nose away
has a long history in damping down
social disorder. The first rich man
who fed it to the poor, so they say,
was the Inca, who liked his folk to stay
content with little. Then he lost his crown
to the next rich man, the Spaniard, who kept on
the good custom that from day to day
made them want less; killed their appetite.
The next rich man, up in Texas, used it
to pay his road-gangs; a happy workforce
being good for business. And the next, of course,
got rich through you, who paid his price and bought
what he chose to sell, as a good peasant ought.

Sometimes

Sometimes things don't go, after all,
from bad to worse. Some years, muscadel
faces down frost; green thrives; the crops don't fail,
sometimes a man aims high, and all goes well.

A people sometimes will step back from war;
elect an honest man; decide they care
enough, that they can't leave some stranger poor.
Some men become what they were born for.

Sometimes our best efforts do not go
amiss; sometimes we do as we meant to.
The sun will sometimes melt a field of sorrow
that seemed hard frozen: may it happen for you.

Torturers

So the grandmothers walk, softly, but their black
outlines are hard in the sun, to the big house
of the president, and they demand the children
of their dead children. In voices like ash,
white and brittle, they explain that the torturers
from the last regime, when they had quite finished
playing with someone, and put them away
for good, would not infrequently find
infants left over, and would take them
home to their wives: loot.

The president is a humane man,
and not a little intimidated, besides,
by the vast loss frozen in their faces,
and he says, certainly he will try to find
what's theirs. (To bring the torturers to account
is proving beyond him; where's the evidence,
the witnesses are dead, and anyway
he'd lose half the army.... But to give back
the old women's grandchildren is justice,
for once, at a bargain price.)

So here and there, in a comfortable house
in the suburbs, some boy tries out
a new name on his tongue. The man
he has been calling father forced the screams
from his father; planted the electrodes
in his mother.... And carried him home
to feed; play with. He tries saying: torturer,
but fails, because, when you come down to it,
torturers are human like any other men,
and this man loved him.

She was nineteen, and she was bored

She was nineteen, and she was bored
with being a kitchenmaid, cleaning a house,
being nobody. She joined the murderous crew
of mediocrities out on the loose

after revenge. They gave her a uniform
and high black riding-boots; no housemaid's gear,
and a whip, and enough authority
to look in most faces and see fear.

She was head wardress; she had the word,
people lived or died at her option,
and mostly died, because, given power,
she overdosed on the exhilaration

of misusing it, of seeing her betters
at her boots: where's your brains now, eh,
your education, your class, your fancy job,
your money? She spent five years on a high.

She could have followed other roads to fame:
she might have been a heroine, a Joan,
she might have been noted for character
or wit, or courage, or compassion,

if she'd been intelligent, large-minded,
but she was neither; she was a failure
born and bred; an ignorant slut, which didn't stop her
being dissatisfied, taking what adventure

she saw. She was hanged young, as she deserved,
it's no excuse that she did what we might.
Those who made her world are still in business:
the likes of her are no nearer the light.

Because

Because our police are not averse
to setting dogs on scared working-men,
we should complain loudly when yours cut loose
with whips and guns, smiling through your pain.

Because we can be turned from any place
where our masters don't wish us to go,
our gorge should rise when you show your pass,
as if we were humiliated, too.

Because rich are so estranged from poor
that they might be of another nation,
we should flinch when your short-sighted neighbour
rebuffs you out of incomprehension.

Because things aren't yet that bad here,
we should reflect that they might grow worse;
that your rulers aren't subhuman either,
and might once have been turned from their course.

There are invasive plants: you let them in
a corner of the garden, and the root
runs underground; its nature is not seen
till it takes over: tyranny is like that,

suffer it a little, it will soon grow.
To rate your freedom cheap lowers the price
of ours: what we think good enough for you
is what will be good enough for us.

I am Roerek

I am Roerek: I was king
of a little scrap of Norway;
large or small, I would not part
with what I had.

I fought a man whose luck
swallowed mine; he blinded me,
but being a good Christian,
he wouldn't kill me,

just kept me about his court,
where I spent my spare time
earnestly attempting his life.
After the third try

he said: don't you ever give up?
and shipped me to Iceland.
I stayed a winter with this man
and that: we always quarrelled.

Now I lie under a hill,
hear the muffled wind shifting
over the grass; uneasy,
like the sea in a shell.

I am the only king
to lie in a land too stubborn
for kings; an edgy country.
It suits me well,

for I am one who would not
co-operate; tailor my wants
to fit reality. Roerek: king
and cosmic nuisance.

Railway signals

(Welsh Industrial & Maritime Museum)

This is a good place for those things to wait
whose use is over. It ends a wide street
going nowhere: artery of the failing trade
whose handsome derelict buildings were left stranded
by the ebb-tide; banks, exchanges,
chandlers, all quietly minding their lost business.

Inside the museum, the old machines
wear fresh paint. They still work; piston-engines
drive nothing round, running smooth as ever,
pulleys lift air, boilers supply power
to nowhere in particular. Outside,
a pilot cutter settles in the weed

within sight of the sea. The tide's out;
between the moorings, wooden piles jut
from the mud, each bearing a railway signal.
Nothing about them is exceptional
but their place; caught out here so far
off the rails, they look a little spare,

at a loss even, but so do most
of the exhibits, for they *are* lost
in a special way. The use is gone, you see;
it isn't like Roman jewellery
or suchlike, for that could be in use
again; the owner's dead, not the purpose.

But what's here is as far obsolete
as only modern industry can get.
What it did is being better done,
or not at all. A discontinued line,
last week's Top Thirty, last year's video game.
It moves aimlessly in the same dream

as the facades of the dead businesses,
staring up the street with their empty eyes
at the new houses for the new people.
Things have moved on; things are unsentimental
like that. You can't force the world to need you,
and if it doesn't, there's nothing much to do

except wait civilly while a layer
of nostalgia distances you, like a picture
behind glass. There will be a curious grace
to your stance, out of context and purposeless
as it is; pointing the way back,
watching the litter left in the tide's track.

Dieppe: Sports Day

When the rehearsals started to go wrong,
troops landing miles off-course, boats lost
in the fog, we all told ouselves: it'll be
all right on the night. There wasn't one
of us translated those fluffed lines
into deaths.

> *There wasn't one of them*
> *who'd seen a battle, give or take*
> *a few officers with long memories;*
> *they'd been training for months, making*
> *successful landings around Portsmouth,*
> *learning nothing.*

We couldn't see the beach
for smoke at first: then when it cleared,
we saw a steep shelf, and a sea wall
laced with barbed wire, no-one told us
about that, and gun emplacements
everywhere, and we looked at each other
sideways, and thought Christ,
this isn't much like the Isle of Wight.

> *It wasn't much like the reports*
> *from intelligence, the ones that said*
> *it was lightly defended, no wire,*
> *and they wouldn't know anyone was coming.*

They were firing at us from the cliffs,
we couldn't see them; it was just a few yards
to the wall; a bloody obstacle course:

we were dodging, swerving, crawling,
I shut my eyes and thought: this
is unreasonable, it's dangerous, someone
could get killed. And when I looked
again, there was a whole company
just lying in the open, like they were tired
after a race; why don't they take cover,
oh Christ, they're all dead.

Nine hundred
dead: another two and a half thousand
captured or wounded. Next morning
the Hamilton Light Infantry went on parade,
all ten of them; the Royal Regiment
mustered thirteen.

They took prisoners
in droves; men sitting crying
among the corpses. When they marched us
away, we were so tired; throats dry,
empty inside. I remember thinking
maybe they'll give us tea and biscuits
for effort, like after sports day.

A shipwrecked Inuit learns Gaelic from a Hebridean

When he comes in, he smiles; waits for your face
to answer him, then reaches out
to touch your shoulder. You speak
the name he calls himself: Mac Cruimein;
his face lights and he nods, says it slowly
for you to get the sound right. His names
for things are softer than yours, and they blur
at the edges; change shape on his tongue
all the time. The one who keeps the fire,
who goes softly in and out with food,
the one you call *arnuk*, he calls her *ban*
and *bean* and *bhean*.... At first you didn't guess
they were the same word; now, you wonder
by what law they change. His language
is like a code to you; you file
his words away against your own, translate
each time you listen. Meanwhile
you read what you can: the different tones
of his voice; gestures; the gentleness
in his hard hands. You are becoming fluent
in him; you know what makes him laugh,
what weather worries him, what way
he has to make a living. His woman
tends your wound; already you're beginning
to think of her as *ban*; it sounds natural
because he says it. The time is not far
when you will feel the word shift on your tongue
by no law, except what rings right
to you, as it does to them. Their soft speech
will shape your thought; change the appearance
of things you knew. And your old words,

filed away, will stiffen; grow unhandy
on your tongue, if you don't take care
of them. It's hard to keep a language
without you see it on a man's face.

(Suggested by an (imaginary) incident in a short story by Farley Mowat.)

What a way to go

You could be Aeschylus: touch your fire
to a line of images, beacons leaping alight
across space and time; you could go as near
to truth as words can reach; then you stroll out
and some careless fowl drops a tortoise
(I ask you), in passing, and there's your skull smashed.

But it doesn't have to be as bizarre
as that. A little too much fat will do
to harden the arteries; a little tar
silts up the lungs, and the machine won't go.
Or you could keep fit and live healthy,
and take a few years longer to die.

What a thing is a brain, after all:
how intricate its roads; what a journey
it can map out. How universal
its concerns; how timeless its memory,
housed in a structure like a Friday car
built to fall apart in a few years.

Sometimes you look out from some hill
over fields clouds roads, the smoke of houses,
over light and distance, weather and travel,
and think: who will ever guess
what moves in me; what thoughts spend
a dragonfly's day inside my mind.

Because your name doesn't need to be
Aeschylus: you could be called Fred,
and you'd still not be ready to die,

nor have answered the end for which you were made.
The problem's this: we're all of us
irreplaceable, and none of us will be missed,

and it's a waste, and what's to be done
about it? Alchemy didn't come up
with the goods; paradise is out of fashion,
and something sometime's going to put a stop
to all you are, without a by-your-leave.
Aeschylus and a few others have

the consolation of leaving a name,
and that's about all that does last,
which seems a poor prize in a risky game,
but since it appears to be the best
on offer, one might perhaps venture
quite a lot to achieve it before

the tortoise happens down. It's some motive,
at least, for gentilesse and gallantry,
and we shall not know how many live
better than they might, because they will die,
and if that seems small comfort for being dead,
no-one gave more to Aeschylus, or Fred.

An even worse way to go

He lies and waits for death to come near,
since mercy's face is masked, and medicine
is handed at arm's length. Which of his kin
would kiss him: which friend share
his sheets? His gaunt face is the fear
that walked the plague years, when the vermin
left the ships, and love wasn't in,
and those died who thought first of another.
He never knew there was so much space
as the vast black hole of aloneness
where he lies collapsed. He used to favour
casual contacts, brief warmth: he avoided
sleeping alone, in the short time he had
before he'd have to sleep alone for ever.

A modest request

I don't ask much: just wish I could have been
Christopher Marlowe; cried the great lines
at a stunned audience dizzy and hurting
from the wordfire, senses shot to hell,
wondering how words could be so violent.
'See, see where Christ's blood streams in the firmament.'

Just wish I'd been half as dangerous,
as quick, as insufferable to all
who didn't like to be pricked into thinking:
just wish I could have been so awkward
to satisfy; so restless after knowledge.
'That like I best that flies beyond my reach.'

Of course, I would have modified the lifestyle;
blasphemed in private, left the boys alone,
kept out of knife fights, watched my words,
not that they would have needed much watching:
I see they would have discomposed no man
'What is beauty, saith my sufferings, then?'

Cameraman

You must see all suffering,
all cruelty, all injustice, all pain:
you must fix your eye on the starving,
the tortured and the executed: you
must look away from nothing.

You must not turn your hand
to feed children, nor to caress
the dying, nor to defend
victims. You keep the lens
in front of your mind,

that others may reach
into pockets, knock on doors,
dig wells. You are the itch
in others; you can make them
see clear, if only you watch

exactly; if you record
just what happened. Do not be tempted
to turn the camera inward:
your stricken looks are no concern
of the public's. They need the word

on what you saw, not how
you felt. It is they who must feel
they saw it; they were there; so
involved, they condemn somewhat
the remote likes of you.

Tulips

The tulips named for your home town
bloomed well for me this May.

The weather was kind to them:
no wind bowed them down,

and though for a long while they lay
under snow, they came through;

they were winners. They did their name
honour; they had shape and class.

They were not unlike you,
without the pain and the weakness

that make us care so much more
for a man than for a flower.

TRANSLATIONS

SIMON DACH (1605-1659)

Letzte Rede

Last words of a once-proud Lady
on her deathbed

Poor bag of worms: but a few weeks are gone
since I walked straight and supple as a deer,
greeted by many friends, honoured and fair,
and now I lie stretched out, all skin and bone.
Was this the thing I once hung gold upon?
My limbs waste, and my sight is just a blur.
I stink, friend: hold your nose and don't come near.
Oh Christ, how is my arrogance brought down!
Come ladies; come young folks: make me your glass;
learn here the worth of beauty, pride and class.
You see my life is done, and I must go.
Farewell and know yourselves; live prudently,
remember what a fright death made of me.
I do but lead the dance: you're coming too.

ANDREAS GRYPHIUS (1616-1664)

Menschliches Elende

The Misery of Being Human

What's a man, then? The dwelling-house of pain,
a jack o'lantern, ball that chance has tossed,
a stage of fear, where suffering heads the cast,
a melting snowfall, a light on the wane.
Our life's like a brief chat, fleeting and vain,
and those who've left the flesh in which they dressed
and entered death's long casualty list
are from our thoughts, as if they had not been.

As lightly as a dream, yet with the force
of some great river, changeless in its course,
so do our name and praise pass out of mind.
What now breathes air must vanish with a breath,
what's not yet born will follow us to death,
and we shall be like smoke on a strong wind.

Grabschrift Marianae Gryphiae, seines Brudern Pauli Töchterlein

Epitaph of Mariana, his brother Paul's baby daughter,
who died at one day old when her family fled as
refugees from the town of Freystadt

I: born in flight, breathing the smoke of war,
ringed round with fire and steel, my mother's care,
my father's fear, was thrust into the light
as my land sank in angry, burning night.
I saw the world, and soon I looked away,
since all its terrors met me on one day.
Reckoning by days, I wasn't long alive:
count up my fears, and I was ninety-five.

151

Dominus de me cogitat

When I was young and easier to hurt,
in my spring days, sorrow became my wear;
death orphaned me. Sickness began to tear
at my soured flesh, and I was made the sport
of misery, a master of the art
of grievance. Every prop that you would swear
was solid, gives beneath me. I must bear
my grief alone: there's none to take my part.
Yet no: God's eye and hand are on me still.
He's fired with fatherhood, and I can fill
his heart: he cannot help but care for me.
When men can find no means, he finds a way;
our strength may fail; his powers never may.
Where most I thought him absent, there is he.

Ebenbild unsers Lebens, auff das gewöhnliche Königs-Spiel

A likeness of our life, after the game of chess

Time plays with man, and with his time man plays:
on this world's board he sits uncertainly.
One climbs, one falls; one lives in poverty,
another lords it. Fortune turns all ways:
there is dead wood where green leaves used to be.
What was, is not; poor stranger guests are we,
and from a thread above us, the sword sways.
Of the same flesh, but not of the same blood,
one walks in velvet, one stoops in the mud,
till Death the robber strips us equal down.
Play this grim game, while Time is so inclined,
but know: leaving the board, you leave behind
wealth, wit and honour with your borrowed crown.

PAUL FLEMING (1609-1640)

Bei einer Leichen

On a corpse

Thin mist when the winds are swift,
flashing light across the sky,
showers that leave the ground still dry,
gunshot, a brief smoky drift,
echoes in an empty cleft,
storms that threaten, quickly die,
bolt that finds its mark truly,
ice in sun, and nothing left.
These are things we well may call
empty and ephemeral,
but, as swiftly as they pass,
so your life, oh man, flies hence,
prisoner of transience.
All is nothing: you, its glass.

CHRISTIAN HOFMANN VON HOFMANNSWALDAU (1617-1679)

Lob-rede an das lieb-wertheste frauen-zimmer

Poem in praise of the most amiable of womankind

Most precious ladies, sunshine in our mind,
choice jewels who adorn our streets and houses,
what man of stone is hostile to your kind,
you conquerors of everything in trousers?
When all your beauty's wares are on display
who'd stand before you; who so bold and mighty?
To such divinities who would not pray,
the living likenesses of Aphrodite?
However, I shall only touch upon
two of your charms; my senses' ship has landed
on those soft shores where waves of milk are blown
by none but love's light breeze.... To be quite candid,
it's breasts I have in mind; those marble hills
where love's pavilion rises up and topples
at a mere breath; on which the sun's gold spills
its perfumed light. They are those Eden-apples
which every Adam longs to nibble at,
a pleasure-park, two cliffs caressed by zephyrs,
a crystal spring whose streams are honey-sweet,
a pure white altar where the whole world offers.
Two sisters sleeping chastely on one pillow,
two armouries for Cupid's ammunition,
a kindling that can warm the coldest fellow,
a lime that holds the senses in submission.
Unheard-of wealth, cordial to cure the dead,
rubies in alabaster, honeycomb

where weary souls lick sweetness, the good bread
of heaven, love's stars lighting the wide room
of space. They are a sword, hacking deep wounds,
a winter-blooming rose-bush; they're an ocean
on which poor sailors hear the siren sounds,
two snowy Aetnas lit by sparks of passion
that melt hard steel. A pond of silver fish
to sate love's appetite, all pleasure's tinder,
a wreath where virtue blooms, youth's only wish,
a blaze of snow, a pastime and a wonder.
They're love's round coffin, key to every heart,
the seat of joy, flowing with milk and nectar,
two decoy-birds, that trap free men for sport,
two brilliant suns that blind the rash inspector
even through mist.... They are a dress of silk
so thin, that you can see each threadlike vein,
two chalky hills, two churns of fancy's milk,
two purest wells that never want for rain.
Two hunters, who trap in and out of season,
two snowballs women aim at poor men's peace,
two snares, too subtle for the sharpest reason,
two stalls on which the wares of love and grace
are on display; wares that no merchant can
acquire, except his lips would be the banker,
two market-baskets full of marzipan
after whose sweetness thirsty mouths will hanker.
Two noble towers of ivory where Cupid
stands sentry with his bow, two gems that gleam
on women's bodies as they fool men stupid,
a bellows fanning an eternal flame.
Ruby and pearl, met in a marriage-bower

where almond's milk washes the rose, its neighbour,
a sea-compass that bids the weary rower
pull like the devil to gain pleasure's harbour.
Love's throne, glazed lily-white, a sacred shrine
where hearts kneel humbly down and chaste lips kiss,
a sea of joy and sensuousness, a mine
of diamonds.... Tell me, why should you screen this?
Why cover such a useful pair of globes
and hide the latitude of love's own country?
Oh beautiful; believe me, all your robes
can't cheat the keen glance of a loving sentry.
The lighthouse of your breast gleams through the mist
of silk you wear, guiding some lucky sailor
into love's harbour where he takes his rest
while I'm still storm-tossed, busy with the baler.
It's well for him who lives so at his ease,
who hides from grief, with that white shield for warden,
who feeds on milk and honey all his days,
who sits at leisure in the lily-garden,
who gathers flowers in a snowy meadow,
who mines the rubies from the richest lode,
who plucks the roses out of the thorn's shadow,
who has the sweet strong apples for his food,
whom fortune loves so well, it calls him brother,
who loves the breast he makes his pillow of,
who flies, unhesitating, to his lover
and floods her with the liquid balm of love.

Auf eine übersendete nelcke

On the gift of a carnation

You send me your mouth's redness, and it comes
clothed in this flower that is your messenger.
I see the white field, and the blood that blooms,
but where's the warmth? That never came with her.
I honour her with kisses past all counting,
—I can't do less: I had her from your hand—
but I don't feel the liquid fire mounting;
spirit and heat she does not understand.
She cannot bathe my mouth in a warm flood,
she has no tongue to probe me tenderly,
she does not paint my mouth with my bright blood,
no sudden bites to thrill and frighten me.
No subtle pulse to prise my lips apart,
no quivering heat gives savour to her kiss,
no teasing moisture; she has not that art.
Spirit, blood, sap: all these in her I miss.
But yet my mouth, unwilling she should go,
lends her its moisture; kisses her with fire.
Ah friend: wish me the moment I want so,
when your abundance may sate my desire.
It tears at me, a sweet anticipation,
a memory of what your mouth can do.
Give me a kiss to go with this carnation
and show the flower can't compete with you.

Ihr hellen mörderin'

Bright murderesses

Your eyes, bright murderesses, douse their fires,
but still your shapely breast,
the tinder to my lust,
gently respires.
The avalanching snow summons its power
and blows my flame to flower.

I think your very breath must be of flame,
for that which swells with it
seems to be all alight.
The ruby gleam
of buried fires touches the peaks of ice
and warms my fantasies.

You sleep in peace, while I lie waking here,
lost in a teasing maze
of lustful thoughts.... I gaze
inside me, and you're there.
My bruised mind seeks to ease itself, and so
it kisses you.

I feel how, even here, the sweet emission
of musk that comes in me,
when your tongue probes acutely,
floods me with passion.
I wish your sleeping spirit might feel what
my fancy is about.

For if you did, a good dream of wrongdoing
would go right to your head
and force you to a deed
beyond your knowing,
a deed which, when you'd finished with your dream,
would make you blush with shame.

The god of love, as grudging as you are
yourself, draws down the blind
to shut you from my mind,
so sleep well, dear.
But you must tell me honestly, at last:
are these dreams to your taste?

Mein hertze schmeltzt in einer stummen glut

A secret fire

My heart is melting in a secret fire
of which no spark is suffered to escape.
The very smoke is stifled; buried deep,
and silence chokes the burning of desire.
Nature has made me worship a bright eye,
and the law calls my longing infamy.

Is it a crime to look too fondly, then:
what sin is in a kiss, a harmless laugh?
Am I supposed to tear myself in half?
God understands the hearts and minds of men.
Love is His child, and He will never damn
as theft or violence our mutual flame.

What man can make himself other than human,
or live a saint on this earth anywhere?
Flesh cannot hold from flesh: no barrier
will make a longing man keep from a woman.
The angels sinned in heaven, as we know;
then how should men stay angels here below?

Though Sylvia be locked away from sight,
forbidden fruit is always twice as sweet.
The byway, not the high road, lures our feet,
and out of pain and danger grows delight.
The sweetest nut may have the hardest shell,
and though thorns hurt, the rose is valued still.

Oh Sylvia, I don't know where I am,
I can't tell anybody how I hurt,
nor name the pain that's tearing me apart
while the self-righteous try to kill our dream.
If you take pity on my state at all,
look at my deep wounds; put your hand in; feel!

You know how, in this world's malevolence,
our faults are reckoned up by one and all,
how men make sport out of their neighbour's fall,
seeing his flaws, never his excellence.
Spin a dense web of lies to be my cover,
that the false world may not find your true lover.

And if you do, surely a musk-drenched kiss,
perfumed with everything that's rich and sweet,
will soon refresh us in our desert heat.
Great flood, break quickly where our famine is!
I think that Love Himself will laugh above,
to see two tongues that cannot speak for love.

JOHANN PETER HEBEL (1760-1826)

Auf den Tod eines Zerchers

Epitaph of a drinking man

They've just buried a man I knew,
and now his special gift's lost, too.
Search where you like, you'll never find
a man like him: one of a kind.

His hobby was astronomy:
in any town where he might be,
he'd search the houses, near and far,
hoping to see a *Sun* or *Star*.

He was a daring hunter, too:
in every town that he passed through,
he'd always start by finding out
if there were any *Lions* about.

He was a proper Christian man:
when he was staying in some town,
each night, discreetly, without fuss,
he'd go, a pilgrim, to the *Cross*.

The gentry loved to have him stop:
a *Duke* has often put him up,
indeed, he had the kind of charms
you look to find in a *Queen's Arms*.

And now he takes his rest, dead dry,
as, some day, shall you and I.

Die Vergänglichkeit: Gespräch auf der Strasse Von Basel zwischen Steinen und Brombach, in der Nacht

Transience: a conversation on the road from Basel, between Steinen and Brombach, at night. A father and son are driving home in an ox-cart

The boy says to his father:

"You know, Dad, when Rötteln Castle looms up
like that, nearly every time, I can't help thinking
of our house ending up that way.
Just look at it: doesn't it send a shudder
through you, like that figure from the Dance
of Death in Basel? You get more scared
the more you look at it. And our house,
why, it sits square as a church on the hill,
light in all the windows, couldn't be finer....
Honest, Dad, will it ever be like that?
It just doesn't seem as if it could."

"Oh, but it can, then; that's a fact!
Things come new: folk start young; old age
creeps up on 'em, they all come to an end.
Nothing stands still. Don't you hear the water
rush by; don't you see star after star
up there? You'd think none of 'em stirred,
but they're all on the go, everything is.

Oh aye, that's the way of it, you needn't look
like that! You're young still: well, so was I,
but I'm not now. I'm getting on, all right,
and if I go towards Gresgen or Wies,
fields or woods, Basel or back home,
I'll end up in the churchyard just the same,
like it or not, and when you're like me,
a grown man, why, I'll not be there;
sheep and goats 'll graze over me,
that's a fact. And the house isn't getting
any newer; the rain soaks it shabbier
night by night, and by day the sunlight
blackens it. There's worm in the woodwork,
ticking away; rain gets in at the loft,
wind whistles through the cracks.... And now you
close your eyes, too, and it's your grandson
mending the old place. But in the end
the rot 'll get a good hold, and then
it's all up with the house. And by the year
two thousand, say, every house in the village
has fallen in, all gone to ground.
Why, where the church stands, and the mayor's place,
and the parsonage, they'll be ploughing
one of these days —"

                    "Oh no, come on!"

"Oh aye, that's the way of it, you needn't look
like that! Isn't Basel a likely town?
Why, it's got houses, I've seen many a church
not so big, and there's more churches

than houses in a village. Any amount
of people, and money, and fine folk,
and many a man I knew, been lying now
a long time asleep in the cloister
behind Cathedral Square.... And no help
for it, lad, one day it's all up
with Basel: all gone to ground.
Well, maybe here and there a limb
showing still: a beam, an old tower,
a gable. There'll be elder growing,
beeches in one place, pines in another,
and moss, and fern, and the herons nesting
—poor old place! — and if folk then
are as daft as now, they'll be seeing ghosts,
the White Lady; she's at it already,
so I've heard tell, and headless horsemen
and God knows who.... What's that nudge for?"

"Hush, Dad, keep it down till we cross the bridge
and get past the hill, and this forest!
Haven't you heard about the savage huntsman
who haunts here? And look in the bushes
down there, that must be where the girl lay,
the one who sold eggs, that was found
half-rotted, a year back.... The ox knows,
just listen to him snort!"

                              "What, our Laubi?
He's got a cold, that's all! Don't talk
so silly.... Get on, Laubi: you too, Merz!
And you: let the dead be; they'll do no harm

to you.... Now what was I just saying?
Oh yes, about Basel falling down.
And some travelling man years from now,
half an hour, an hour's ride away,
he'll look across, if the weather's clear,
and say to his friend that's beside him:
'Look, that's where Basel was! That tower
was St Peter's, they say: shame it's gone!' "

"Oh no, Dad, you're joking, it won't happen!"

"Oh, that's how it'll be; you needn't look
like that! And there'll come a time, the whole world
will burn to nothing. A watchman will walk
at midnight, a stranger no-one knows,
bright as a star, calling: "Wake up, wake up;
the day's here!" And the sky turns red,
and there'll be thunder all round, quiet
then loud, like the French cannonfire
in '96. That'll shake the ground!
The church towers will rock, the bells
will sound for service, all by themselves,
and all the world'll be praying. But come day,
God help us, we won't need the sun,
with the lightning, and the earth in flames.
And there'll be more yet, too much to tell,
but in the end it'll all catch alight
and burn and burn, all the land, and no-one
to put it out, and how will things look then?"

"Oh Dad, I don't want to know any more!

Except — what'll happen to the people
in all that burning?"

                        "Why, they'll not be there
when it goes up, the people: they'll be —
where'll they be? Never you mind: be good,
live a decent kind of life, wherever
you are, and do what you know's right!
See how bright the sky is with stars?
Well, what if every star's a village, ·
and further up, further than you can see,
a great fine town like Basel? You behave
yourself, you'll end up in a star like that
and have fine times, and if it's God's will,
you'll find your dad there, and your poor mother.
If you drive right up the Milky Way,
into the hidden town, and take a look
back down, what'll you see? Why, Rötteln Castle!
Mount Belchen and Mount Blauen, all charred
coal-black, like two old, fired towers,
and in between, nothing but scorched earth.
No water in the Wiese, all bare and black
and dead quiet, however far you look.
So you see that, and you say to your friend
that's beside you: 'That's where the Earth was,
and that mountain used to be called Belchen.
And not far off was Wiesleth: I lived there,
spanned my oxen, carted logs to Basel,
ploughed and drained and cut wood and lived
my little life there, till the day I died,
and you can keep it!' — Get on, Laubi, Merz!"

Acknowledgements

Some of these poems and translation have previously appeared in *The Anglo-Welsh Review*, *BABEL* (Munich), *The Hutchinson Book of Post-War British Poetry*, *National Poetry Competition* antholgies for 1987 and 1988, *The New Welsh Review*, *The New England Review*, *North*, *Pequod* (San Francisco), *Planet*, *Poetry Society Anthology 1987-88*, *Poetry Wales*, *Poets Against Apartheid*, *Snooker Scene*, *The Western Mail and 2 Plus 2* (Lausanne).

'Inter City Lullaby' won the Cardiff Literature Festival International Poetry Prize in 1989, and 'M.S.A.' the Welsh Arts Council Long Poem Competition in 1988.